BLACK SHEEP

TOSHIKA

Honestly speaking or should I say writing , i have no idea whom I should dedicate this book to . Maybe I should dedicate this to the people who showed me that trust is not a cheap thing to just give away to everyone or maybe to the people who changed overnight . Maybe to those who pretended to be worried about me but really it was just their image i was tearing up by question their unjustified rules or maybe to those friends who turned into bullies making me hate myself and giving me insecurities when actually they were just jealous they were not me . Actually I should thank all of them because without them I wouldn't have felt that sadness and that never ending loneliness. And if I hadn't felt that I wouldn't have started writing.

"So cheers to all of them and many more to come this one's for you......."

Contents

Contents

Foreword

My father also likes to write . His poems are mostly about politics and love . Two completely different things . I believe that I got this liking in writing in my genes I'm not gonna say talent because you haven't seen my work yet nor do I have feedback of someone I think is capable of giving me an honest and useful critic . I have no idea what is going to happen to this book but I do know that whatever I put in it will be something out of heart not just my mind .

When I was around 12 or something I wanted to become a writer . I used to look at stories and poems in my school books and under the title would be the name of the writer . I always wanted to see you name there . I wanted to know how it feels when you see someone reading your stories or poems . I dropped that idea when I got know that my father had higher expectations from me . But god had some plans for me so here I am writing a book which he don't know about i might add .

I initially started writing to get emotions out my heart and onto a paper because sometimes feelings become so much of weight that it is not possible for one to keep them inside anymore . It made me feel that whatever I felt is not inside me anymore and it is heard by someone . It made me feel like I'm standing on cliff and screaming my heart out for the whole world to hear.

Preface

I don't have any experience in writing well I have written above 40 songs that I think are amazing. Don't worry you'll get to hear them one day too . I want to become an actor which I sure as hell will doesn't matter how much effort or time it will take . I like playing with emotion . No...no..no.. not in that way . I meant using them in art. I like to think I'm a very artistic person . I like dancing , singing and acting . Well that's the reason I'm the black sheep of my family .

The pharse black sheep of the family is rather a very old saying . In 18th and 19th century when sometimes a black sheep was born in flock of white sheep and because it gave black wool and black wool cannot be dyed it was useless . It was also consider as bad luck and a mark of devil .

I'm not going deep in this because you can easily find this information on Google which is where I got this from . I think you are here to know my views so here they are . Cambridge dictionary says that this phrase means a person who has done something bad that brings embarrassment and shame to his or her family and I believe that is load of bullshit . Well I think that being a black sheep means that you are the person in your family who will change the stereotypes forever . Let me tell you something if you don't fit in than you don't need to fit in . You were never meant to fit in. God made you to bring some changes in world and you will do just that . You are that person who you family line was waiting for even though they don't know it yet . Someone who takes stand and don't back down . Someone who has courage to stand for themselves when everyone and everything is against them . It takes guts to be the black sheep and if you have the courage the world will be yours .

Acknowledgements

I would like to thank notion press for making this process so simple and free . I always wanted to publish my own book but one thought that held me back was what if no buys my book and getting it published will be hell of a work . Honestly saying I didn't even knew how you get your book published . Well the reason or should i say excuses are never ending but now I have this platform that is helping me write this book down and cannot be more grateful. Thank you so much to the whole team.

Prologue

1. Rumor

Rumor has it
She was buried under the castle land
She was a queen unknown
Keeping her life on stand
When she rose
She rose like a phoenix at the very hour of dawn
She looked so radient
Her gaze was rays of sunshine
It lit hope in human which it fell upon
Rumor has it
She was slaughter in cold blood
For being one of a kind
Or maybe men couldn't take in the fact
That she asked questions they didn't liked
Their was a knock on the door they heard a thud
She was not forgiven for the truth she brought in world
She knew this risk when she walked on this road
She gave a promise to her daughter
And she had to keep her word

2. What we are

Soon there'll be sun
And night will fall apart
Sun rays will touch your skin
And it'll make you spark
Maybe people think you have no worth
But that's not for you to worry
Actually it's the last
To know what we are
Is to know that it's just the start
'cause you'll change
No way you'll be the same
If you don't evolve over time
You'll be out of the game
Seriously it's not that hard
But it's important for us to know
What we are
Whatever are your perspectives
Make sure you believe them
Not because someone forced you to
If you don't have them yet
That is cool too
Take your time
You have all in the world

But the moment you stand for something
That something should be your right
It should be something
That's worth a fight

3. Daimond heart

The heart which goes through some shit
They hammer it day and night
Hit hit hit
Know that they are found in mines
And before you find one
You have to face a bunch
For you to win a fight
You have to learn how to take a punch
There are People who change skin
More times than a snake
You need a eagles eye to know what's fake
You might wanna give up
Or maybe go back the way you came
But what if you get to know later
All you had to take
Was one step
One move and you'd have it
It'll be a new start
Then my friend you'd have a diamond heart

4. Friendship

Is it still friendship
If i don't feel safe with you anymore
If i feel like I'm walking on eggshells everytime I'm around you
That i feel I'd be better without you
And i don't know if the next joke would be about my body
Or face
Or how i talk
Or how i walk
Maybe you will push me from the stairs and laugh as fall
Maybe it will become a funny story
That you'd like to tell
Maybe you'll slap me in front of all
And say you couldn't control your anger
You really think that because it's been a while i shouldn't remember
How do you expect me to treat you when you shower me with stones
This isn't what friends do
And if it is then I'm better alone

5. Practical minds

Little crocked on the side
See colors of rainbows
But they remain white
When they fall from the cliff and reached the rock bottom
And that's how
They became practical minds
Trust broken uncountable times
Walking with their heads down
Even though they were right
Feelings were soaked out of their souls
And that's how
They became practical minds
They see through they façade
Once they couldn't see
Even in the darkness
They shine bright
Only few can understand
How they became practical minds

6. Perspectives

When we wake up in the morning
We know that dream was lie all along
Doesn't mean you stop dreaming
You just gotta stay stong
People don't wanna listen
They just wanna talk
Even in the worst of all hearts
There is love hiding under some rock
Sometimes you have to take the path that is wrong
Sometimes you have to sing a different song
Sometimes it's not easy to let go of Things you planned to hold on
But for your own good
You gotta go on
Thinking things differently
Make them different
You see the glass half filled or half empty
It depends on how you fill them
Fill them with sorrow you'll see half filled
Fill it with happiness and you'd think
Shit half got spilled

7. Claim

You try and put your claim on me
When you lost it ages ago
You make decisions for me
You never take my no
We ended the moment you changed
You think you are my weakness
That was a year ago
Now you are my pain
You are like a old fashioned curse
That don't go away
The moment I look over my shoulder
I see you standing at the bay
I won't lie no one can fill your space
But this is it
There's no more of us
This is the end of our days
Maybe in next life
When you lose your ego
We'll be together as one
Till then i rest my case
And i think I'm done

8. Just a boy

I'm just a boy
Who live down the alley
Heard some noises
At my neighbours house
They sounded deadly
Asked my dad what was that about
He frown and said without a doubt
Stop getting coy , you're just a boy
I saw the neighbour's woman
With a black eye
Maybe i stared too long
But she looked like she wanted to die
Her skin looked pale
There was dried blood on her nail
She looked like life was sucked out of her
But she managed to smile
Kinda looked fake
I went up to her
Asked her few questions
She had a sad smile she said
I feel like I'm a toy but who am i complaining to you're just a boy
I don't know why is everyone silent

When they can't see
They pity her
Pray for her
But no one's settings her free
why can't I do something
I feel pathetic that I'm just a boy

9. Sometimes

Sometimes we lose people
We love
Sometimes they lose us
'cause they think we weren't enough
Sometimes we mostly
Walk on the harder side alone at night
Sometimes we'd give anything
For a ray of light
Sometimes it becomes so much
For us to hold on
We lose our grip to make it hurt less
Sometimes we aren't able to clean up our mess
Sometimes it's not easy to think about everyone else and not us
Sometimes you go through happy days
Other time they are rough
Sometimes it's better to let go
'cause you're both tired from holding up

10. I live for what ?

In journey of life
We meet people all along
Some tell secrets to rise
Some to fall
This world is yours to save
It is mine and it is yours
You can turn your back
because people will never understand
Or you can play song in your head
When they talk nonsense
Say the word
Don't be shy
If you know you are right
Then you are right
Doubt will get you nowhere
What will be difference between you and others
If you don't even believe
You can stand your ground
Or can decide to leave
You have one life
And one day every one will die
You can either do what people want
And regret the very last day

Or you can do what you want
And die with a smile on your face
People will curse you either you help them or not
This is the truth
So ask yourself
I live for what?

11. Truth or lie

Scream on top of your lungs
People won't belive your truth
Whisper a little lie on there backs
They will believe it is true
If this isn't reality then what is it
'cause all i see is that
You live a beautiful lie called life
No one wants to talk about death
We know the truth
But convince ourselves we don't
It's easy to ignore something like that
Then to face the real foe

12. Why me ?

Let me answer this question
In simpler words
You can relate with it doesn't matter a jock or a nerd
Pathetic rhyming that's was
But i want to write it
So whatever
These words will be here forever
Back to the answer
That is 'cause you can
It's simply two words
I know that
But know it you won't be given something
Unless you have the power to own it
So more the trouble
More strong God thinks you are
This isn't some exam you can cheat on
You give the test first
And then you get the lesson
So you mr or miss or mrs
Need to make this confession
How many times have you used these two words "why me"
I have a question for you too
It's easier than your

Why say why me
When you can say you know what life
Try me .

13. Family

Why are you looking at me
Like I‘m an alien
I am a human , i have perspectives
Do you expect me to not talk
Why do you want me to close my heart with a lock
It doesn’t make sense
You are supposed to support me
Instead you went ahead and made this image
Do you loathe me ?
We love each other
Then why can’t you accept me
I accept everything about you
But you just want to perfect me
Don’t you like me the way i am
When I was young
You used to say I’m special
Now all you care about is for me to settle
I don’t want that life
I like to take risks
Why do you think that I'm a broke thing
That you need to fix
Can I ask for love ?
Can I ask for care ?

Can I ask you to be by my side ?
No you say
It's not fair
If you don't who will help me
Aren't we supposed to be family?

14. Loved ones

Dear loved one
You will always be mine
But you know this works two ways
So far the working part is mine
You gave me a warning
Labelled it as love
You know there is no love in that kinda stuff
You hate who i am
But still say you love me
And I'm forced to say it back
You can't even tell my favourite color
Am i supposed to understand ?
You are amazing
And I'm too
But i just thought this through
We are wonderful people
Just not for each other
So say it last time I love you
And I'll say i love you too

15. God's plan

Who are you to interrupt
All mighty's plan
He want you to become great
And that's exactly what you're gonna get
Don't get caught up in all intoxications
He planned a long life for you
Don't bother calling those toxic people again
He threw them out of you life
'cause they deserved to.
You know he'll always be by your side
Wherever you are standing.
He is not your lord but your friend
He is genuine, don't like pretending
You believe in him , he believes in you
That's how it works
You do the best you can
Hard work has it's perks .
You are going to change the world
And you know it
Believe in yourself 'cause he does
You are one in a million
And it's time you show it

16. Daughter to my father

He was my first love
Only friend i needed
The person i cared about the most
Maybe that's why he left without a scar
While i bleeded
I would've burn the world for him
In a heartbeat no question
He was my art
He was my passion
My world started and ended on him only
But he had other people in his life too
He left me there
Now I'm lonely
He was my oxygen
And i thought i was his
But he changed over a night
The moment I grew up
He wasn't the same
Now i was just his daughter
I guess i didn't fit in the frame
Never had i ever thought
This time will come
Where we will end

He was my everything
But i was just a daughter to my father

17. Sarcastic sorry

Narrow minded people, like to be stable
Don't get we aren't like them
They don't get real just like their fear
Creeping out from their heads
It's funny how they justify everything with one fact
We love you and won't want anything bad
Oh I'm sorry did my back hurt your knife
Oh I'm sorry was i not easy to convince
Oh I'm sorry that i made people question you
Oh I'm sorry what I said out loud was true
I'm so sorry

18. The girl who lived by the river

The girl who lived by the river
Committed suicide
She hung herself from a tree
There was a rope with which she was tied
They look at her way
Always says she was so weak
They murdered her over and over
'cause she was unique
Her parents took shame upon her
Her friends made fun
They all shook their heads in sync
When her chapter was done
She spent her whole life
Looking for just one person
Who will be by her side
She search through the day
But then came the night
She was nothing more than object to this society
They say it was a suicide
But i think we all know the reality
She died everyday for years
Now she only put an end to it

She must be so depressed and devastated to do it.
You'd thought people around her would change after this
But they only loathe her more
Tell me society what do you want
You've taken so many
How many you want more

19. Mistakes

Mistakes we all make them
But they aren't something we aren't supposed to do
They are just apart of life
Nothing to be afraid to
Someone who knows the right thing to do
Must have know the taste of wrong
It is something that you learn from
So learn to be strong
You fail then you learn
Then you succeed
'cause now you know what to do
And even if you don't that time
You are just in for another lesson
Life teach you until you pass the test
When you do
You become better then the rest
So put your hand on your heart
Say it's ok to make mistakes
You don't have to Panic
It's for your own good and
The experience you'll take
People will talk shit about you
Even if you do nothing

So don't look just jump
'cause that dive will look stunning
My friend , make mistakes
It's your right
You my dear were born to fight

20. Goodbye

I'm fed up with your style
It never brings us together
Two days of peace
It never stays forever
Our roads are different
And we are just in each other's way
We try to change it
But at the end we pay
If this is what life wants
Then we have to give in
Maybe in different life
Will have the same route
We can drive together
Can play our song on loop
But right now it's a farewell
I wish you all the luck
I hope you move on too
And don't get stuck
If i say I'll always be here
It would be a lie
It's time my love , goodbye

21. Human thing

If you make the same mistake
A thousand times
It's human thing
It's not easy to be brave
So if you fall apart
It's a human thing
We don't choose our fights
We just choose if we are gonna take it or not
Sometimes life seem like an end
Other times it's alot
It's a human thing
It's ok to ask for a break
It's human thing
It's ok to sometimes fake
It's a human thing
If someone don't expect you to be a human
It's a human thing
To get emotional over small loss
It's a human thing
Be who you are and don't be so hard on yourself
Don't worry if you overthink alot
It's a human thing

22. On the top

Just think how you'll feel
When this will all works out
When you will have that dream figure
You'll have your dream house
All the things you wanted so bad
You will sleep with peace in your head
Everyday you'll do something you love
People can talk
You won't care
You are above
Waking up in Morning with excitement
And a smile on your face
Let me tell you something
Even then you'll have your fights
But you'll just be a better fighter
You'll know the moves to make
You'll hold your sword tighter
This is the start and you'll run till you can't
You'll know how it's like to be the person you dreamt to become
On the top of the world with a crown you deserve .

23. Sunrise

Do you ever get the feeling
You can't tell why
You know you messed up and it's a lie
Being alone can be amazing
Unless you are crying
It's too much to wait up for tears to dry
I don't want to be in this shadow
That gives me nothing but disappointment
I know i can rise
To reach attainment
It suck when there's no one to pull you out of the train wreck
These shadows surround you
So you can't get back
But i will get up
And I'll see the sun again
I won't give up to these
Mere excuse of men

24. Good at being a girl

They say I'm not good at anything
I can't look good
Or please people out of my comfort
I can't cook food
Or make sense out of absurd
I try and try to be the person they want
But when I try to ignore my inner voice
It feels like a taunt
My face is melting
With the heat of their so called rules
It's gotta be fun to brag between the fools
But finally I found out
What I'm good at
And this it's a movie so i won't twirl
Listen carefully, i won't repeat
I'm good at not being a girl

25. Let go

Cut the people out who make you feel bad
They won't stop unless you stop giving them chances
They know you love them
So they will make advances
You know you want to
But you fear loneliness
It's better to be alone then to be with
Bunch of wolves
Who will kill you for you flesh
So take this risk
And let go

26. Motivation

Don't look outside
Motivation is inside you
If you want something don't ask
Win it , the worrier is inside you
Don't look at someone's body
Look at yours for the motivation
You don't have to lose weight
'cause she has an healthy body
You have to 'cause you don't
And you want it bad
Believe me after you get through
You will be glad
Inside you , you will find
Everything you need
You don't need to cry darling
Nor do you need to bleed
Be there for yourself
'cause everyone else leaves
Be your bestfriend not an enemy
Lead yourself to the victory

27. Soul

When the moon shine
I depart from my soul
I look through me
And i see myself whole
I been here before
I just don't remember
This feeling of peace
I want it forever
This soul of mine overthinks alot
So i leave it sometimes
Believe it or not
They say my dreams are worthless and so is my goal
How do I tell them
I left ' i care what you think about ' soul

28. Win

It isn't in my blood
But i begged you on my knees
You knew you were special to me
You rained on parade
Knowing it will harm me
I still didn't said a word
I let you think it was your victory
Being my friend is amazing
But being my foe is nightmare
You have caused this upon you
Now i have to be fair
You will pay for what you did
It's time to get rid
Of all that's left
I will come back again
And this time I'll win

29. Limit

You are your only limit
No one can break you
You are what you became
No one can make you
Just set you goal
And walk towards it
If someone stops you
They are not your well wishers
Just remember how it feel to be on the top of the mountain
Forget those jitters
You have one life
You don't need to impress
Be your best version
And express
So One day when you are on the death bed
You can smile
You'll know you lived best of your life

30. Black sheep

They call me the black sheep
Maybe it's my nature
I stand out in crowd of cowards
My words are often fatal
They see my courage
Take it for ego
Tell me i won't last
In this battle of people
They say I'm just a big mouth
With an empty mind
But i believe it's better than being their kind
I'm different and i won't have it any other way
And if people don't like it
Well it's just fine
Being a black sheep comes with some responsibilities
Every single step , people test your abilities
They'll drown you in deep waters with a rock tied to your leg
They will slaughter your throat in a second
They'd like to hear you beg
And after all this and much more
The best comes out of the black sheep
And wisdom knocks on it's door
It isn't easy to walk on this path

You leave everyone behind
You go on this path alone
Without knowing what you might find
So my black sheep
Are you ready for this journey ?
You can back out
You won't forgive yourself for this sin
'Cause black sheep are only made for win

Printed by Libri Plureos GmbH in Hamburg,
Germany